Ladybug at Orchard Avenue

SMITHSONIAN'S BACKYARD

For Geoffrey — K.W.Z.

For Lin — T.B.

Book Design: Shields & Partners, Westport, CT

10 9 8 7 6 5 4 3 2
Printed in Singapore

Acknowledgements:
Our ʌery special thanks to Nathan Erwin of the O. Orkin Insect Zoo at the Smithsonian's
National Museum of Natural History for his curatorial review.

Library of Congress Cataloging-in-Publication Data

Zoehfeld, Kathleen Weidner.

Ladybug at Orchard Avenue / by Kathleen Weidner Zoehfeld ; illustrated by Thomas Buchs.
     p.   cm.
Summary: Ladybug rambles through the garden, up and down rose stems in search of her
favorite food, aphids, instinctively using her natural defenses to escape from threats.
     ISBN 1-56899-257-2
1. Ladybugs — Juvenile fiction. [1. Ladybugs — Fiction.]
I. Buchs, Thomas, ill. II. Title.
     PZ10.3.Z695Lad 1996   95-45892
     [E] — dc20   CIP
                                               AC

Ladybug at Orchard Avenue

by Kathleen Weidner Zoehfeld

Illustrated by Thomas Buchs

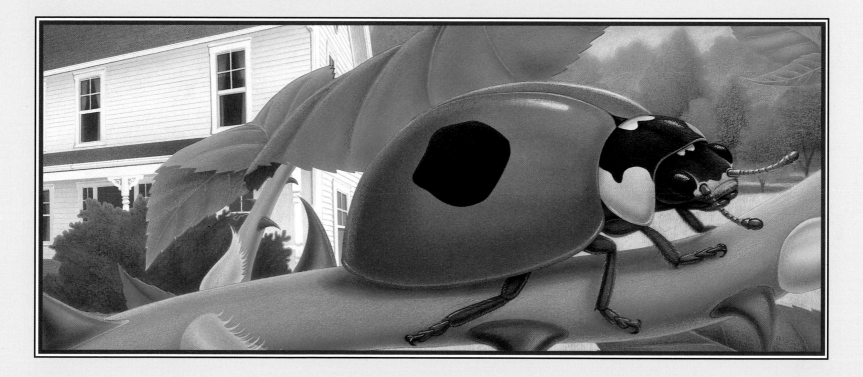

Soundprints

Where Children Discover Nature

The bristly jaws of an ant gape over Ladybug's head like a giant pair of pliers. Ladybug's jeweled eyes see only a dark shape towering above — probably just a twig.

She creeps forward on the cherry leaf, searching for food.

An autumn wind blows through the
cherry tree. The branches tap tap tap against
the white clapboard of the house on Orchard
Avenue. Ladybug feels the leaf rocking like a boat
in a stormy sea. Tiny claws and sticky pads on her
feet hold her fast.

The ant looms closer to her.

Intent on her hunt, Ladybug waggles her antennae.
She touches the familiar shape of a little green insect —
a sweet, juicy aphid. She opens her mouth for a bite.

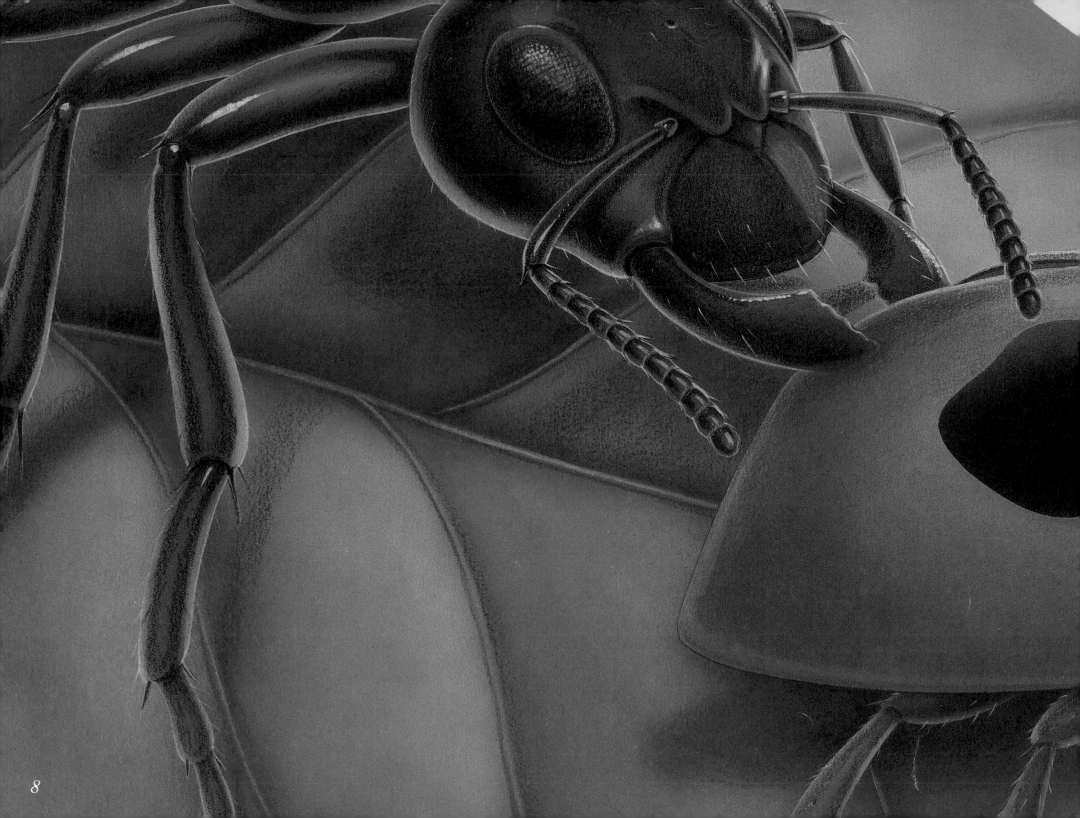

Suddenly the ant strikes down on Ladybug's hard red forewings. She feels the thud of its big jaws. Her forewings protect her — for the moment.

The ant is determined to defend its herd of aphids. They give off sweet honeydew — its favorite food. Ladybug dimly sees the ant raising its head again.

9

Ladybug leaves the tasty
aphid and retreats. She flees
down the cherry tree on
her dainty claw feet.

On the ground, she struggles over two mountain-sized pebbles, then discovers a rose stem. Up she climbs, ready to hunt again. Cold weather is coming, and Ladybug must eat and store fat for the long winter ahead.

As soon as she reaches the top of the rose stem, a wren lands beside her. Ladybug feels the stem bob under the bird's weight.

The bird cocks her head and studies Ladybug with one eye. Ladybug does not notice. But her bright red coloring warns the bird that Ladybug will not taste good. The wren decides to eat a nearby aphid instead.

The wren's beak jabs at the aphid like a dagger.
Startled by the motion, Ladybug pulls her six stick legs
tight against her flat black belly. A smooth little hemisphere,
she slides off the leaf and drops to the ground — belly
up — legs still tucked. Blades of grass tower around her
like skyscrapers.

The grass rustles. A hungry mouse steps near. Ladybug does not move. She oozes a foul-smelling yellow liquid from her leg-joints. The mouse sniffs Ladybug and scurries away.

When all is quiet, Ladybug waves her legs in the air. She pushes hard with her forewings and turns over. Then she marches through the grass city, until she comes to the next rose stem. Up she climbs, ready to hunt again.

She follows the vein of a leaf, wagging her feelers before her. Again she touches an aphid. She smells its sweet fragrance. She tries to grasp the insect in her jaws. But before she can, the aphid raises the rear end of its body and gives off a blast of sticky fluid in Ladybug's face.

Frantically, she scrubs her face and antennae with her front legs. Her antennae and jaws must always be clean so her senses stay keen for hunting.

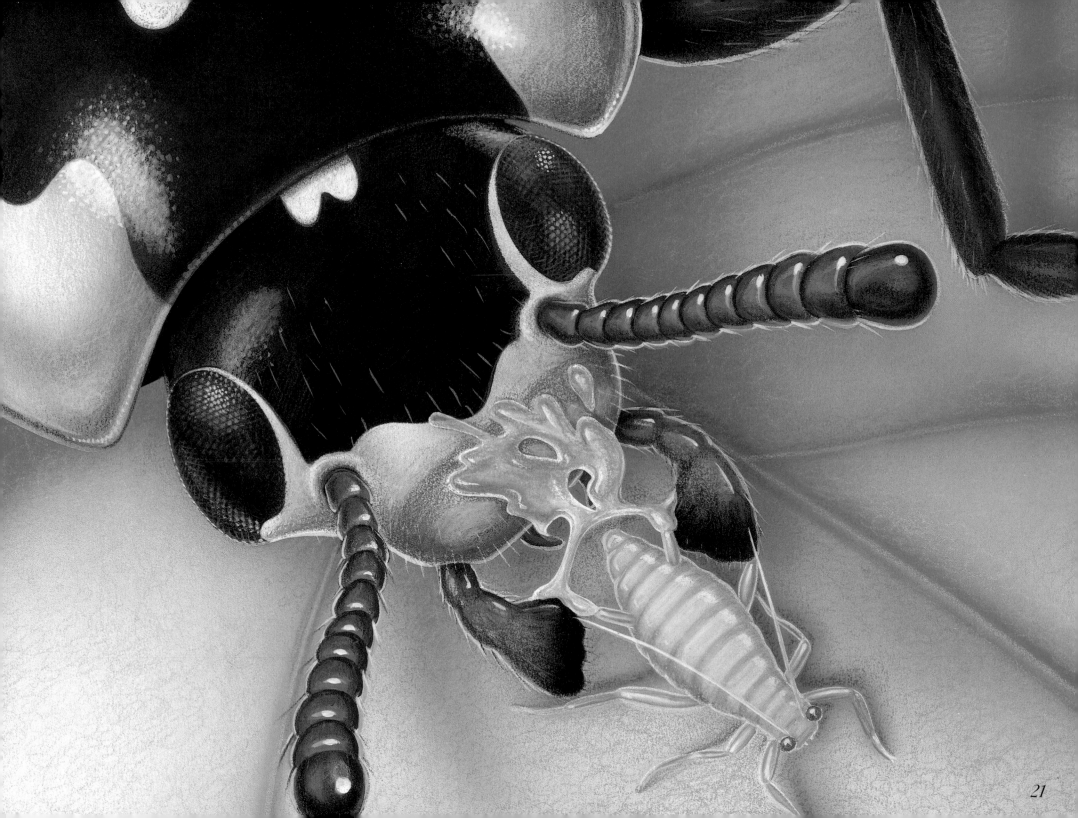

21

Scrubbed and tidy, Ladybug wiggles her feelers. She walks around the leaf in little circles, still hungry for aphids. She loops back again and again, examining every bump on the leaf.

At last she finds another aphid and seizes it. She chews it up and then moves on to another — then another and another.

Finally, Ladybug is full. The aphids she has eaten will be stored as fat. The fat will be her only food for the winter.

As the sun begins to set, Ladybug stands motionless on the leaf. A chilly wind rocks the rosebush. Ladybug feels her joints growing cold and stiff.

On the stem above her, the aphids have laid eggs that will hatch next spring. Now, one by one, the aphids die in the cold. The ant returns to its home underground. In the sky, the wren starts the first leg of her journey to the warm south. The mouse finds a hole in the foundation of the house and moves into the cellar.

Ladybug climbs to the top of the rose stem. A few needles of icy rain begin to fall. She lifts her red wing cases.

27

With wing cases held high for balance,
she unfolds her lacy black underwings.
Up she flies — up to the bedroom window of the
white clapboard house on Orchard Avenue.
She settles on the windowsill, folds her wings, and tucks
them neatly under their red enamel covers.

Ladybug wanders around, sluggish from the cold. She probes with her feelers until, finally, she discovers a tiny crack in the window frame. She squeezes herself in.

And there, warm and cozy, she will sleep for the long snowy winter.

About the Ladybug

Most ladybugs, also known as ladybird beetles, are predatory beetles that feed on aphids and other garden pests. This story is about one of the most common — the "two-spotted". The ladybug's characteristic hard glossy shell, on which these spots can be seen, is actually a set of forewings, which protects the delicate flying wings found underneath.

While many types of ladybugs hibernate in large groups, the "two-spotted" sometimes hibernates alone, in cracks in walls, behind windows, and even in rooms.

In spring, all ladybugs become active. The females often lay eggs on leaves, stems, or tree trunks. In a few days, the eggs hatch, and out climb bumpy, gray larvae, which look nothing at all like adult ladybugs. The hungry larvae spend several weeks devouring aphids and growing. Then, the larvae attach their tails to leaves or stems and turn into hard-shelled ovals called pupae. After about a week, the shells of the pupae split and adult ladybugs emerge.

Glossary

antenna (plural antennae): the two thread-like organs in front of an insect's eyes used for scent and touch. Ladybugs' antennae often look more club-like than those of other insects.

aphids: soft, pear-shaped insects, much smaller than ladybugs, that sip sap from plants.

forewings: on a ladybug, the hard curved front wings that cover and protect the flying wings.

hemisphere: half of a round solid, such as a ball.

honeydew: a sweet liquid, made up of digested plant sap, excreted by aphids.

wren: a small, brownish bird with a short upturned tail.

Points of Interest in this Book

pp. 4-5 aphids.

pp. 4-5, 6-7 note three simple eyes on top of the ant's head.

pp. 16-17 pin oak leaf.

pp. 18-19 ladybug's lacey underwings.

pp. 22-23 rose weevil.

pp. 26-27 rose hips.